WHAT WE WISH WE KNEW

What We Wish We Knew

By Michael Larson

Ex Machina Publishing Company
Sioux Falls, South Dakota

2005

Cover Art: "Snow Trail" by Timothy Carlson.

Published by Ex Machina Publishing Company
Box 448
Sioux Falls, SD 57101

First Edition, First Printing, February 2005

Library of Congress Cataloging-in-Publication Data

Larson, Michael, 1962-
  What we wish we knew / by Michael Larson.-- 1st ed.
     p. cm.
  ISBN 0-944287-26-3
  I. Title.
  PS3612.A774W48 2005
  811'.6--dc22

                                      2004018496

For Jody

Acknowledgments

Some of the poems in this collection first appeared, some of them in earlier versions, in the following publications: *Great River Review* ("Crows I Remember"), *Image* ("The Games," "The Hunted Man," "Love in the Off-Season," "Raymond of Penyafort"), *Loonfeather* ("My Sister's Secret"), *Mankato Poetry Review* ("Northern Honeymoon"), *Minnesota Ink* ("Protecting My Pawn"), *Minnesota Monthly* ("Receding North"), *National Forum* ("Preparation for Flight"), *New North Artscape* ("After Which the Sadness and Boredom Return"), *North American Review* ("Aquinas at the Last"), *Passages North* ("The Sound of Grass"), *Seeds in the Black Earth* ("Dog in a Parking Lot," "The Furthermost," "Recovery," "Vigil," "When Nurses Take My Blood Pressure"), *Texas Review* ("My Wife Teaching Me about Birds"), *The Christian Century* ("Behind My Lips Like Words"), *The Comstock Review* ("Larsonovic Considers Defection"), *The Other Side* ("A Late Twentieth Century Schizophrenic Considers Gethsemane"), *Wisconsin Review* ("The Dogs Grow Faint"), *Yankee* ("The Parakeet and the Grackle").

A few of the poems in this collection—"Blue Burning," "Notes Toward a Metaphor for Dreaming," and "Protecting My Pawn"—also appeared in the chapbook collection, *The Light Remaining*, published by New Spirit Press.

Several of the poems in this collection have been recognized by various contests: 2002 James Hearst Poetry Prize, Honorary Mention ("Aquinas at the Last"), 2001 Comstock Review Contest, Finalist ("Larsonovic Considers Defection"), 1994 Milton Center Poetry Contest, Second Prize ("Love in the Off-Season"), 1993 Borders/Loft/Minnesota Monthly Poetry Contest, First Prize ("The Sound of Grass").

I wish to thank my mentors, Jim Whitehead, Bill Meissner, Michael Heffernan, and Heather Miller. I wish also to thank my wife, Anne, among many important others, for tireless encouragement and support. Finally, I am grateful to the National Endowment for the Arts for a fellowship in poetry. – Michael Larson

Contents

Intimations

The Sound of Grass 11
Spring Fever 12
My Sister's Secret 14
Saint Cate 15
When Nurses Take My Blood Pressure 16
The Fourth of July 17
Behind My Lips Like Words 18
Raymond of Penyafort 19
Northern Honeymoon 20
My Wife Teaching Me about Birds 21
The Blurred Horizon 23
Late at Night Viewing Slides 24
Larsonovic Considers Defection .25
Dog in a Parking Lot 26

What Others Seem to Know

The Parakeet and the Grackle 29
Crows I Remember 30
Protecting My Pawn 32
Larsonovic Versus the Computer .33
George the Waving Man 34
Angela Merici's Pilgrimage to the Holy Land 35
Bishop of Snow and Ice 36
White Magic 37
The Drinker 38
After Which the Boredom and Sadness Return 39
Man Bent for Bearing 40
The Faltering 41
Blue Burning 42

From Far Away

Lost in the Cosmos 45
Love in the Off-Season 47
Maria and Me 48
The Dogs Grow Faint 49
The Hunted Man 50
The Games 51
Sebastian: Two Deaths 52
Nagasaki, 1597 53
The King of Poland 54
Athanasius and the Champion of the Arians 55
The Gospel Up to Thursday Night According to Mark 56
A Late Twentieth Century Schizophrenic 57
The Furthermost 58

The Night Before and After

Aquinas at the Last 61
Notes Toward a Metaphor for Dreaming 62
Receding North 63
Scholastica and Benedict 64
Your Arms, Your Fingers 65
Funeral at Sunset 66
Preparation for Flight 67
Death Rehearsal 68
On Finding a Saint in a Glacier 69
Vigil 70
Coloring 71
Prescription 72
Recovery 73
What We Wish We Knew 74

The Lord shall smite thee with a consumption, and with a fever, and with an inflammation, and with an extreme burning, and with the sword, and with blasting, and with mildew; and they shall pursue thee until thou perish.

Book of Deuteronomy

Intimations

The Sound of Grass

The water from the cemetery pump
was cold in summer
like Superior, a long drink
for boys hired by deacons
to mow between those monuments
to keep the dead presentable.

I played among the gravestones
after Sunday school,
crouching in their shadows,
looking for my name
under the still pines,
the churchless steeples.

Only once did I bring noise
into that quiet plot
when the hired boy was sick.
Mowing made me thirsty,
made me want to lower my head
into a bucket of pump water
and hear those boats coming
like the sound of grass
getting cut far above me.

Spring Fever

There is something back there
I know. There was the slough in summer
and the tamarack
but that is the wrong season.

There was the dog's casual bark in March
that was a sign of the melting.
There was the long muddy driveway
and popsicle sticks floating the tributaries.
There is a picture of her
in the mud and wearing a pink jacket
and squinting. I love the light

over the driveway.
There was the light over the driveway
some days faintly pink or other-worldly
hues I cannot say.

There were seeds pressed in the ground
under the telephone pole
where the meadowlark spoke
to the mother.

There was the boy finding ways
like leaping off of crates
to jam muddy basketball.
He wore out the net. The boy flew
and his sister loved the mud
and popsicles all year
and in March the sticks were boats.

There were divots the shapes of horseshoes
puzzling the pasture sog,
the green-throbbing grass. There was the dog
who dragged himself back in the evening

after three days of love. That's enough.
There was fever in the sky
and we all caught it. We all died
and let the south wind stroke our hair.

My Sister's Secret

Nothing prepared me
for the bandages,
a stark white wig
enlarging her head,
a girl of the future
as if they had added brain
not taken tumor.
Underneath that gauze
the hair was gone,

a heartbeat skipped.
I folded myself
on the floor
to be like her.

Saint Cate

I've thought about your hair for two days now—
not so much the hair itself but why
you cut if off: to keep the men away.
It didn't work. The men came anyhow
and women too and children. A crowd
converges on your confidence. They try
to understand your clarity, the way
your hands obey the beauty of your mouth.

I think about your mouth now as I watch
the winter kiss those trees across the field.
I wish for once I wasn't on the fence
between my twitch and your eternal stretch
into the woods that burn up as they steal
the sunset blind with bare-limbed elegance.

When Nurses Take My Blood Pressure

I think of a hill on the back of the farm
where I'm drifting away in the knee-high grass.

A dog begins circling. A cloud starts to seem.
The sky is much deeper than I can remember.

The grass moves like water. My scent is a boat.
On a hill, half asleep, I am somebody else.

And because it is summer the pressure is low
and the doctors all say that I'm fit as a boy.

But I know what I know.

The Fourth of July

A nice nurse holds my hand.
Far down the lithium corridor
comes the white-throated priest.
When he arrives, I confess:
"Last night there was a bead of light
blinking about the room."
The nurse blurts, "A firefly!"

The Father shrugs and gazes out the window,
says, "In the distance there are fireworks
barely clearing the horizon." He meant
to say that what bedazzles in the near field
is not necessarily so much from far away.

The rain begins like applause
from thousands of tiny hands.
God bows faintly through the man,
exaggerates the rain with wind, the wind
with rain, unravels in a lightning bolt,
the negative of his descent. He turns
to me and asks, "What do you make of that?"

His hand is resting on my arm.
I cannot speak, he is so strong.
And every mystery is cloaked in one.

Behind My Lips Like Words

I wanted to escape the arms of love,
tall women reaching for me as the bell
took its toll and used me for a tongue,
swung me back and forth above the street.
I fell in this cathedral's vestibule.
Inside the ancient withered priest is draped
with voices of November leaves, a chant
of modern liturgy in monotone.
A hunchbacked widow eats the words alone.
No light breaks upon these pews or stains
the glass behind the alter, eyes of Christ
as big as faces frowning down on us
while we approach. This slow procession makes
for thoughts of requiems. The bodies fade
in brilliant darkness, liquid, thick as oil,
too thick for swimming in but dark enough
to show home movies of our baited lives,
the helpless twitch toward love, the hands we kept
behind our backs to hide what they had done.
I open this black hole for joy which blooms
behind my lips like words unspeakable.

Raymond of Penyafort

Your casebook on confession was a match
rekindling pain. You must have winced to face
the sins a second time, now unattached
to penitential whispering, the voice
of the ashamed, the sigh behind the screen,
the gathering of courage in the dark
undergrowth of grace. How not to burn this scene
in sacramental fire? You peel the bark
slowly. You take away time, ring by ring,
until there's nothing but a core.
Observe again the pulp-soft centering
of soul. Absolve. Turn loose the ghost that tore
the curtain separating us. Show me
the bright face I am not supposed to see.

Northern Honeymoon

Shooting the highway from Grand Marais down
through the midday gray, the sleeping deer.
Doubt like a shadow falls over my eyes
peering in at the edges of timber, trying
to see deeper than driving allows, looking
for her face beyond where the detail stops
and greenery blends with the lack of light.
Although she sleeps beside me now, I search
for her among the dark firs further out.

The fleece creeps in by accident
from across the border where I imagine
unrelated signs for God to send as promises
that only death will part. I made up a deer
out from sleep to race my car and win.
It is only a game I know until my breathing
jerks as the gray doe lopes along the edge
of the woods, parallel to the highway, springs
over that fallen tree and bears away my shadow.

My Wife
Teaching Me about Birds

Grackles descend
on the small feeder.
"It's not normal," she says.

I watch them watching each other,
a fine yellow rim
around every black eye.

Twenty empty half
her supply of millet
within minutes.

"Scare them away," I say.
"But I can't," she sighs.
"It's a bird feeder."

Two dance and flap
toward each other. Neither
will blink.

She shakes her head
saying, "I wanted
to show you real birds."

Their song is the opening
of many old doors;
their feathers iridescent.

"Don't worry," she says,
an edge in her voice.
"They'll all go at once."

I nod and see a cardinal
in evergreen boughs, waiting
like an ornament.

The Blurred Horizon

You will live longer than I
as women seem to have the knack
for living. Though I don't want to die
it's not the death itself
that makes me drink this night.

It's you asleep in the next room, miles
from here, and your habit of watching me
in the mornings while I sleep far away,
a face you can hardly recognize.
It's how we try to recognize each other
and how the square of world
out my window will remain unfamiliar.

It's fifty years from now: me
sitting in some room, staring,
you in another part of the house,
working with your hands. I might call out
sick with nerves, thinking *This is over now*

after all. And you would come, absorb
my shaking, still the false alarm.
I might remember years of arms
hauling me in and lift my stare
over your shoulder, try to focus
on the blurred horizon of the world
I had somehow missed.

Late at Night
Viewing Slides

In this one she is younger
than I, an infant then
in her arms. Her neck
is not arthritic yet
as it tilts her vast face
squarely onto the wall.

I am reaching for her mouth.
Her lips interest me
when they move, tell me
what I will be, what I was.
The past is no less hard to know
than what will come.

My mother's eyes entreat
the camera, which is me,
with their dark light.
And I am blinking still
against the flash. It is so bright
and fast.

Larsonovic Considers Defection

So all I have to do is nod my head?
That's it? The woman by the door will see
and make the necessary phone calls? Gee,
I always thought it would be easier said
than done. I think about the books I've read
that make it seem so dangerous to free
oneself. I always feared the KGB
but maybe they don't even want me dead.

I see the boy I used to be, the walks
around my father's state-owned farm. The snow,
like wheat in summer, glows. I hear the talks
I used to have with God, who has to know
this fear, about the way his careless hawks
would spot me in the fields and let me go.

Dog in a Parking Lot

Through aisles of videos I walk:
breasts, cops, devils, death—
Jesus. I cannot find
the film to start my pulse
so leave empty, wag my serious head
under high stars, duck into my car.

A truck pulls up beside me. In back
is a large smiling retriever
whose eyes are familiar
in the half-light,
whose laughter is contagious,
who barks me back to life.

What Others Seem to Know

The Parakeet and the Grackle

Summer mornings through the screen door
he watches wild birds at the feeder,
twists his head when any of them sings—
bluejays, cardinals, chickadees—he knows
none of their songs so utters his own,
though he is on the side of the screen
which is irrelevant.

He does not like the mourning dove.
If it drops down he screeches, dances
backward, walks a tight circle, cursing.
But if the great black grackle comes to feed,
this parakeet leaps into the screen.
The grackle's call is like the parakeet's
played at half speed, an ancient hinge
which opens unthinkable doors.

Crows I Remember

1
The crow explodes
from a yellow ditch,
steadies his wings,
the arms of a tightrope walker,
eases into long hypnotic flaps
and calls lazily out with the voice
of a man mocking a woman.

2
I think about them
in high-noon sun, gliding
into washed-out landscapes
as if black were the only real color
and they the only solid bodies
to transcend the tar mirages,
the cars that just miss them.

3
I've seen them in winter,
sourceless shadows, absolute
against gray and white,
followed them across crystal air
until the beat of wings
in front of the sun
shattered everything.

4
Smaller birds converge on crows
who fly away unhurried,
who pull stuffing
from the eyes of scarecrows,
who gather together like memory
circling up and up
slipping out of the world in flocks.

Protecting My Pawn

My dog had a vision I could not see
but I trusted his stance, rigid legs
and trembling body leaning hard
against the edge of the natural world.
I believed in the uncertain snarl that slipped
from his throat, his confused bark
at the darkness shrouding the fireplace
where the seer had been the week before,
sensing death left behind in the bricks
by the mason. The dog stood stiff
between hatred and fear and could not attack
and could not return. My human hands
stretched into that chasm, took hold
of the shivering body, understood
as far as I could understand. "Good
dog," was what my fingers tried to say.

Larsonovic Versus the Computer

The Master is beyond intelligence.
He has no need of it since every move
contains Larsonovic's worst nightmares.
Here comes The Master's black bishop which pins
Larsonovic's knight against his queen.
It's sad, he thinks, to be so vulnerable
so early in the game but he plays on
against what has become more than machine.
There is a bitterness between them now:
they'd sooner die or be unplugged than draw.
Larsonovic would even rather lose
and always does unless he hits the key
that starts a new game automatically.
Larsonovic is smirking when he says
"I'm sorry, but it was an accident."
The Master gives no answer as he waits
with glowing green intensity to pounce
upon Larsonovic's new errors.
Brute calculation is formidable,
a million boards a second passing through
the circuits, taking every human thought
to logical conclusions far beyond
original intent. Larsonovic asks
himself: Is this my fate, to play the game
against my bad ideas to the end?
Is there not some move I have ignored,
some plan, some sacrifice that would escape
all calculation, leave The Master lost
forever in improbability?

George the Waving Man

It's hard to see the dragon slayer, shifting
among the winter shades of consciousness
like shadows over lake ice. He gives
himself to myth. That is the only gift
he has to give to us who turn adrift
along this century of science. He rides
a horse beside the freeway, weaves and glides,
implies a question: "Do you need a lift?"

But you don't need a lift. You've got your car.
It's fast and goes wherever you descend.
And come to think of it, you never saw
that rider in the ditch. You're not that far
gone. You never saw the waving hand
get small, the puff of smoke, the last hurrah.

Angela Merici's Pilgrimage
to the Holy Land

They got as far as Crete before she lost
her sight. The others thought they should go home.
What was the point? A holy shrine or tomb
was nothing without Angela. They crossed
themselves and turned to go; she made them stop
and said, "The blind press on and we will comb
this desert for the child that made us come
and I will wrench some meaning from this loss."

By force of will she loved what she could not
see: ancient markers, rocks, an olive tree.
Then on the way back home, in Crete again,
her sight returned. She laughed at how she'd fought
to hear the secrets of Gethsemane
among the mindless chatter of a wren.

Bishop of Snow and Ice

The Pope made me the legate to the North.
I worked in Hamburg thirteen years.
Then Northmen burned my fears
to death.
I had suspected that my work was worth
about as much as ashes, smears
of joy against the jeering
earth.

Now I don't have to wonder anymore.
I'll tell you this: I love those pagans, eyes
like ice, fierce jawlines, utter disregard
for my apostolate. The screams they wore
about their faces chill me in reprise.
It is my name they form: Ansgar! Ansgar!

White Magic

The Guelphs had theirs. The Ghibellines had theirs.
A symbol for each faction of the day.
And that does not include the secret wares
of wizards and their followers. The way
to get ahead in advertising is
to burn an image in the viewer's brain.
An expert logo-maker can undress
ideas into shapes and letters. Strange
how shapes and letters sell us what we want
or what we wish we wanted or at least
what someone wanted. Bernardine was haunted
by this power, so he undressed the Christ
in Gothic letters, wrote him on the sun
so as to burn a hole in everyone.

The Drinker

Summer nights he'd drag us to the drive-in,
make us drain a mug with him and then
he'd have another. Once he started
none of us could stop him.
We'd watch his sweaty Adam's apple
rise and fall with every swallow.
The setting sun would cast the glass
in bronze, in which memory hardens
and he is neither quenched nor thirsty.

After Which the Boredom and Sadness Return

My neighbor rakes in dusky light.
Two aged sweaters drape
on bent and bony shoulders.
My window frames him
with cinematic nuance. Background music
meanders from the front room.
Guitar says everything
through real depth in the screen.

My neighbor is a star.

The film fades into dark. No credits,
no outline of him left.
The record ends. The needle
hisses after the song, after the sun
like the sweep of his rake.

Man Bent for Bearing

My neighbor's back was like a nonsense dream,
his torso aimed forever parallel
to the hard ground, yet he never fell
forward. His troubled posture made life seem
long. And narrow. An endless balance beam,
a slow routine in staying vertical
and God the judge and he an infidel,
a corner in the squareness of God's scream.

He was an open jackknife in my mind.
He was the possibility of blood
if one should fall. He bore the evening sky
upon his back in stacks of firewood
about to burst in flames. I don't know why
he did not falter there where he half stood.

The Faltering

My sister lost her balance once
for no apparent reason, nearly fell
into a street of traffic. A passing car horn
tore away twenty years of faith
in her legs. Now she sits reclined, staring off,
squinting as if she can no longer trust,
as if she knows what she cannot see:
any moment now out of the darkness
will come the spinning red light.

Blue Burning

The hospital corridors are hers.
She doesn't want them, doesn't want
the calm voice of nurse,
the hypo collapse, the dream faces
of ICU.

Just before this second surgery
she clung to me as if
I don't know what.
So part of me went with her
down to pre-op. Hours later

the afterlife: there is that moment
when her eyelids—blue burning
behind them—fight to open, fight
to shut. She is trying to wake up.
She does not want to.

From Far Away

Lost in the Cosmos

1

What if the world had come to Percy's door
for cure? What if they believed
the books, the rumors of something out there
big enough to not get lost
in dilated pupils of a century gone mad?

2

Six weeks before his death by cancer
I was there at the end of his lane
in Covington. A sign said
No Trespassing. I didn't know

he was sick. The priest
had warned me only of the dogs.
The sun set as I could not go on
unannounced or worse, unwelcome.

3

There is little consolation for the lost.
The dreams I dream, in which he seems
to recognize my dream, are only dreams.

4

When Foote and Percy, young men,
drove on a whim to Faulkner's house
Foote went in, conversed all afternoon.

Percy waited in the car, rolled down the window,
read a book, repeated to himself,
I do not know that man.

5
I keep thinking how the dark
might have made it hard for both of us:
I might have been some apparition of the age
and he might have been only what he was.

Love in the Off-Season

It's misting in Eureka Springs this winter night.
My wife and I are standing on the top veranda
of the empty Crescent Hotel.
A hundred years ago the sick stayed here
believing local water would heal

what ails. Now it's tourists
and only in summer. They climb
the narrow zigzag streets searching
endless gilded gift shops, closed today
when we made soft spray on the sidewalks.
We never saw another car.

From this height though I can see many roads,
headlights piercing a thin veil of fog.
I think of children sleeping in back seats,
their parents speaking in low voices.
I think of accidents on nights like this
when limbs and fear go hurtling through the air.
Separately my wife and I both worry. Across the
            valley

a well-lit statue of the Christ
appears to be floating. Arms outstretched
he looks friendly, triumphant,
ridiculous. Above us the moon is
a pale wafer. Just below, there is the glinting
Spanish-tiled roof of a Catholic church.
And they keep claiming that Christ lies inside
broken and bleeding beyond recognition.

Maria and Me

There was that life we had among the fields.
Maria says we loved it just enough.
Is that the reason we are saints? It feels
too simple. Earth was easy on the touch:
the soil beneath my feet, the seeds between
my fingertips, the rain against my face,
the sun against my heart. Where is the pain
in that? I am not smart, I know, to place
my sanctity in question, but I fear
a possible mistake. Maria says
that I did miracles among the poor,
providing them with food. I think she jests.
I barely put my hands behind the plow.
The next thing I remember is right now.

The Dogs Grow Faint

The hounds next door are wailing
again, hunting in cages.
My neighbor raises them for money.
I know by how thin they are,
by the way they shrink under my hand
as if my fingers were knives.
I stretch across that fear
and touch the ear of a walker
bred to run all night. He shudders
and whines and eyes the hammer
hanging from the cage.

In my bed I hear the howling
stop, dog by dog, and see
my neighbor with his hammer poised
above those teeth and skulls,
above the long sad voices.

One night in the heart of his woods
my neighbor will be listening
as the dogs grow faint, speeding away
into the darkness, searching.
At first he'll not quite comprehend
when far-off baying turns around,
those lean beasts coming fast,
a familiar scent in their nostrils,
a muted ring to their voices,
the sound of metal hitting bone.

The Hunted Man

Wounded in the high jungle, he emerged
on the plains. He is leopard-tough,
all spots and sinews in the tangles
of the one tree. You can hardly see him
there behind the leaves
but once you do your hackles rise
toward the unsentimental eyes: they don't change
even when the heart explodes somewhere behind
and the limbs relax one by one
and the sight grows old over you as the rains
begin. And you wonder about the nine lives,
about the garland of leaves about the face
that will not go away, the fixed gaze that is just
between a corpse and a pounce, between a myth
and the calm unveiling of eternity.

The Games

Apparently Perpetua was not
the main event. They had her head cut off
before the others faced the lion's rough
approach, the cruelty of his zigzag trot.
Or maybe they were showing her respect
by not exposing her to that slow death
gazelles have known. She had by rite of birth
a Carthage noblewoman's dialect
with which she had recorded slaughter-fests.
Perhaps it was for this her head should roll
to where she saw the lion tear her friends
apart. She saw the hunger of the beast,
the number of his ribs. Beyond the wall
there was applause, a sea of tiny hands.

Sebastian: Two Deaths

1. Arrows
The first one feels like nothing happens. Whiz.
Your atoms almost part for head and shaft
which seek clean entry. You want to laugh.
It tickles. Blood materializes: this
is how you know you are unfortunate.
Suddenly you see that several more
have found your flesh accommodating, four
to be exact. You count them as you wait.

2. Clubs
This hurts from first to the last, although the last
hurts less. It still hurts though. You want to cry
like when you were a boy. The blurry sky
gives up on you. In darkness you can taste
the iron in your blood. You smell the waste
of your release. You hear a lullaby.

Nagasaki, 1597

In one day, twenty six were crucified.
It was a marathon of martyrdom
on Holy Mountain. Paul Miki was one
of them, a Jesuit, a native hide
nailed fast against the sky. His body dried
in mid-sentence, as did the others'. Sun
above the city caught their lives undone
by thirst, the blood escaping from their side.

Among the dead were doctors (they dressed wounds
that would not heal), Franciscans (they heard crows
pronounce their names), old men whose spacious
        minds
embraced their pain like tired arms around
a corpse, a child whose clear eyes winced and saw
the sun explode into a blinding wind.

The King of Poland

It's too much to expect, too dangerous
to ask a child to conquer Hungary,
to play the strategist when he just wants
to be a saint. He seeks the awful tree
whose fruit creates a deep insomnia.
All night he prays the wind among the leaves.
And when he sleeps, he sleeps on dirt and straw
as if he were a gatherer of sheaves.
His father whispers, "Casimir, wake up.
You are a prince. You will be King some day.
Why are you lying on the ground?" "I hope,"
replies the son, "my king has come to say
that Poland will not fight the wars of men
for I have drunk the victim's blood again."

Athanasius and the Champion of the Arians

All through the night of life, the dead christ stared
at Athanasius who stared back at him.
Neither one would blink and neither dared
to look away or think about the wind
against their faces, sand against their eyes.
The dead christ had it easy: he was dead.
But Athanasius had to squint and cry
the grains away lest they should fill his head.

Still, slowly he was overcome by dust.
When both of them were dead they both stared on
unblinking underneath the morning sun.
The man said to the christ: "I think you must
be tired of this game." The christ said, "Just
a little. And I'm not the only one."

The Gospel up to Thursday Night According to Mark

The walking man was fast. I had to sell
the things I owned in hopes of keeping pace
but even then I only ever tasted
his dust—exquisite dust! I watched it swell
into a storm. Against the wind I fell
repeatedly. Paul says it is a race.
I think it is a falling on one's face.
I think it is a ringing of one's bell.

I shed my tunic in the end to cut
the wind resistance. Wearing nothing but
a loincloth, I got close enough to see
the kiss that brought the walking to a halt.
I caught my breath. Then soldiers surprised me.
I broke their grip and ran for misery.

A Late Twentieth Century Schizophrenic Considers Gethsemane

Sometimes I think I'd like to comfort Christ,
find him in a garden Thursday night,
stroke his hair and wipe his bloody eyes
and say, "It's all right, Jesus. It's all right."
And in so doing I could make amends,
explain that I am not the worst mistake
he ever made, that I would be his friend
if he would not insist I stay awake.

But in the night there is that urgent prayer,
that plea to take away the dreaded cup,
a rasping in the solitary air,
a ragged voice who always wakes me up,
the breath of God still breathing on himself
as I lie screaming, "Jesus! That's enough."

The Furthermost

Once there was a mother and a father
and their billion children, all of whom
had cancer. "You have enough offspring,"
said their wicked servant whose job
was to teach the children to smoke.
"You must think about your retirement."
The mother, still very young, laughed
and the father cried. He did not want to fire
his oldest servant so tore out his own heart
and the mother held it in her hands.
And the servant was appalled because the heart
kept on, showered her in waves of radium,
a fine red mist spreading out across the fields,
settling on the brow of the furthermost.

The Night Before and After

Aquinas at the Last

...and all that I have written seems to me
like so much straw compared to what I've seen
and what has been revealed. The waving sea
retreats. The fields grow still and turn from green
to gold in what can only be described
as everlasting sunset, light that halts
the senses and the mind I tried to bribe
with words and words. But it was not my fault
that I should try: I thought it was my gift
to gather symbols for the things I longed
to taste. I thought with language I could lift
my head into the heavens. I was wrong.
You would agree if you'd seen what I saw:
the *Summa*, though it seems like grain, is straw.

Notes Toward a Metaphor
for Dreaming

Death is the sleep between
the two days of eternity. *Too easy.*

Sleep is to dreaming
as death is to purgatory. *Maybe*

sleep is the death between
any two days of disease. Life

is a kind of malaise
while dreaming about a place.

Receding North

My sister has November eyes
the end of an abandoned driveway
where the last brown leaves
blow by her house
leaning against Canada.

She draws this foreign air
slowly, lets it lift her up
through black wet limbs
to see the North coming
over the curve of the earth
for her.

Wistful she descends,
watches her white breath disintegrate
in trees, remembers other winters
blanketing her with sleep,
a layer every year
on her bed of wind.

She is deep under the covers now
dreaming of how much farther north
the spring might find her,
how much fainter
the rest of us will seem from there.

Scholastica and Benedict

Ben, when your sister says she's dying, you
should listen close. This should be obvious.
Her voice breaks as she begs you not to go.
There is that secret fear behind her eyes.
Don't say you didn't know. You couldn't bend
your little rule a little for your twin? Men
will often love the letter of some law
more than the spirit of their sister. Blink
and she is gone. You reach to close the jaw
and then you understand despair. I think
it would be worse, though, had that storm not come,
the squall that saved you from your urge to run.

Your Arms, Your Fingers

You who wince and grimace day
and night, who crack your eyes on sunlight
when your sister dies,

you whose trail turns again
and again, your circle says, "Nothing
for as far as you can go."

You who found a kiss
could be a hole, who lost your lover's tongue,
words adrift in your throat,

you who prayed and rolled
around but could not shrink
your wound, oh.

You who weep and gnash
among the high pines, who wring
your fingers in whiskey haze,

you whose arms are waving now,
I can see. I feel your blows
as you turn into me.

Funeral at Sunset

As the slow spin
hides us from the sun
our skin turns the color of cold.

But we are not cold.
We are hesitant
about the new color of things.

We try to embrace
the newly dead
with the impotent arms of ghosts.

As the whippoorwill
repeats his question
we tire of the absent response.

Preparation for Flight

This horizon will resolve
in what is whispered
under every storm: you will grow
wild, engulfed, undone inside
the willow grasp. You were impaled

against the trellis of new words
and fences falling back to weeds
that wrap the world around you
like a prayer held in place
by the cemetery's cold tooth.

What you feel in the throat
you swallow like a bird.

Death Rehearsal

I am as far away as clouds
unfurling in the past. There is grace
that sees beyond the wall of sky.

The drone of sun burns white
around my head, a stone from the river
which is far and slim and dark. You break

inside these ribs like joy cracks
in light described by rhythm,
the vernacular of time and sense.

The genuine reflection on your eyes
is of the cantering sea.
It is a lonely ride for you

across the bay. There is the salty wind
reminds me of my purpose. I buy
these intimations nightly from a Jew

and sprinkle them by morning in the sand
where wheat is growing by the surf
inside the wing of time.

On Finding a Saint in a Glacier

We don't know anything about your life.
The ice between us is the streaky window
of time. Striations of the fixed field bend
your boyish face in agony. The whiff
of death still flares your nostrils in a tough
embracing of the Diocletian wind.
At fourteen, death is all you have to send
across the centuries. It is enough.

It is too much in fact for me. My arms
have almost held a dead young woman. She
was not a saint but she was young like you.
Now winter never really ends. The charm
of spring is only that. And all I see
is snow behind the sky's deceiving blue.

Vigil

Why do I keep watch for you? A book
said ghosts appear within the first two years.
After that it's rare. But Thomas says
"a rare bird is rare," and that is all I need
to dim the lights and grow my pupils.
Can you see me on the couch?
I am the one whose head falls
awake, jerks you from his dream,
your purple turban vanishing. Beneath
lay the horseshoe scar. Your hair
would not unfurl. You are
a secret in the world
where I keep watch.

Coloring

The pages of this color book have oxidized.
My daughter's fingers, soft and small, turn
each brittle figure, now a clown, a rabbit,
a sentimental girl: too many curls, too much
dress. My sister's left hand left
this colored wax—*age 4, age 5, age 6.* It hurts
to see that crooked signature
grow steadier. She worked on these
for years, her bright hair falling
on the page as she drew close
to keep the color inside, her fingers white
around the crayon, her lips tight. There it is,
her best work near the end, and then
a few she never did.

Prescription

Walk. Take your glasses off.
Glance—don't stare.

Breathe. Somewhere past your lungs
you find the center of your loins.

Weep whenever possible, the way your children do.
And sleep as if you trust. Allow yourself

to be observed by others in the room.
Pray this way: say "Oh. It's you."

Recovery

Swimming is the cause of all effect.
A glass of water rests in twilight,
is what the river gives. Fishes
multiply and lurk or lie there still.

In picture frames on desert walls
we see the limbs dissemble.
What lies between the bone and skin
is fog, a lyre without notes.

In resurrection I can hear the word
who whispers up the wind
with lips like purple flowers.
This is the first of many gifts

in transit time, where we have lost
our taste for anything but wine
and memory grows white and thin,
the way a scar gives up.

What We Wish We Knew

I. What I Sang to Her

Some questions have to go unanswered.
Some answers are a kind of cancer.
And you been wipin' your eyes again.
And I been watchin' the skies.
And I don't know why it's still rainin' here
But we could drive until it's clear, clear, clear.

II. What She Said to Me

In your myopic eye there is the love
of intimacy. "Stay with me," you say,
your focus always perfect here at twelve
inches, where imperfections of my face
are all too clear. Your lungs fill up with air
according to the history of your
abandonments, the things you lose or lose
yourself in. What the body stores is more
than merely physical. It is your life.
The day you married me is there somewhere
and all the days less strange and more, like when
you had a summer job and someone ran
to your assembly station out of breath
to say there was a problem back at home.
This kind of news is slow to register.
You think about the words and what they mean.
You shake your head as if there is a choice,
as if your sister does not have to lie
unconscious in an ambulance. She does.
She did. Your dad will meet you at the door
and drive you to the hospital. And there
you will begin to comprehend at last.

74

For many years you tried to pray, but "Please"
was all your lips could form. It must have changed
your posture. I don't mind that you are hunched
and broken in the shoulders, even now
so many years after it ended. I
am not at ease myself. And think of her:
the disappearing slowly in the cure,
the hopeless effort to absorb, along
with sorrow's medication, what it was
existence might have meant. You were appalled
by this, her quiet confusion. Your eyes
kept getting worse. I can't remember when
your nosebleeds started, but there seemed to be
no way of stopping them. They ran their course.

The body stores whatever we forget
if we should happen to forget. Your blood
is not original but is unique.
Our blood together gives our children breath
and life. My stomach, streaked with memory
of what I carried, is a thing I try
to hide. I don't know why, except maybe
it is not beautiful. It is my life,
nevertheless, recorded perfectly
in flesh. Our children change us. They write words
between our ribs we can't pronounce. My love,
I look to you for answers you don't have.
What lies beyond this dusky field of stones?
Can we see clearly in a world so full
of miracles? What does our daughter keep
behind the glitter-dark of irises?
You cannot tell me what I want to know.
And I could not have asked for any more.

The Author

What We Wish We Knew is Michael Larson's first full-length collection of poems, many of which have appeared in literary magazines and some of which have earned him a fellowship from the National Endowment for the Arts. He received the MFA in poetry from the University of Arkansas and the MA in English literature from St. Cloud State University. A Minnesota native, he currently teaches English at Minnesota State College – Southeast Technical, in Winona, where he lives with his wife and three children.